'A most wonderful introduction to the intricate designs hidden in science and nature'
Olga Bogatyreva, Doctor of Science and Dr Nikolaj Bogatyrev, Biologist
www.biotriz.com

'… gives fresh stimulation for young brains … provides cognitive encouragement which can increase the desire to learn, to question, and to find logic in the world.'
Dr. Raymond H. Hamden, Clinical Psychologist
The Foundation For International Human Relations,
Washington, DC.
www.fihr.info

'…they [Iya and Graham] have joined forces and created an amazing world, accessible to all, where science and art merge for human contemplation. Maria Montessori talked of 'seeking order' as a human tendency and the pages of this book provide incredible images where order and beauty can be sought to satisfy this human sensibility as well as being a unique resource to seek knowledge of our universe in the micro and macro.'
Anne Shiner, KleinKinder Montessori
www.kleinkinder.co.uk

'This beautiful book is a unique blend of mesmerising images for young eyes and fascinating facts to enlighten any parent.'
Chrissie Weltike, Early years Educator

'The EARTH DESIGNS are a wonderful invention in the world where children are exposed to a vast sea of information, sometime dissonant and chaotic. They [EARTH DESIGNS images] help a young developing mind to tune into the natural harmonics of symmetry, rhythmical patterns and the logic behind the laws of creation. Such visual stimuli will nurture the imagination and appreciation of harmony.'
Maria Danishvar Brown, Painter and Art Lecturer
www.mariadanishvar.com

'I highly recommended this book. You'll love looking at it as much as your baby does and that is so important when encouraging a child's development. There's a lot of validity in the power of black and white images to young babies and this is a really nice way to share the experience with them.'
Laura, Parent in Somerset, UK

'If you want to introduce your baby to the wonders of nature, this is perfect for you… Or if you believe that there are no limits to your baby's understanding and you want to maximise learning potential. There are no other well researched and creative images that I have come across. This is the best. Great start for the baby.'
Adrian, Parent in Somerset, UK

EARTH DESIGNS: Under The Sea

Black, white and red book for a baby and the whole family (from two months old)

First Published by Cosmic Baby Books in 2016

Written and illustrated by Dr Iya Whiteley and Dr Graham Whiteley
Designed by Iya Whiteley and Rachael Fisher
Edited by Daphne and Mark Thoresen

Copyright © Dr Iya Whiteley and Dr Graham Whiteley 2016

All rights reserved.
No part of this publication may be reproduced, stored in a retrieval system or transmitted, in any form or by any means, electronic, mechanical, photocopying, recording or otherwise, without the prior permission of the copyright holder.

Publisher shall not be liable for any activity involving this information or any other consequential damages.

ISBN 978-1-9124900-0-4 (pbk. Black, White and Red)

ISBN 978-0-9935886-3-1 (pbk. Black and White)

ISBN 978-0-9935886-5-5 (hbk. Black and White GIFT edition)

ISBN 978-0-9935886-7-9 (pbk. Colouring book)

Printed in the United Kingdom

cosmicbabybooks.com

cosmic baby books
raising happy children to reach the stars

EARTH DESIGNS under the sea

written and illustrated by

Dr Iya Whiteley

Dr Graham Whiteley

BLACK-WHITE-RED

We give sincere thanks to our family and close friends who have so graciously spared time to help review content and comment on the design of this book. We are very grateful for the kind support.

To our newborn son, Lux, who helped choose the images and to our daughter, Celestiya, who is always keen to colour our images, before we scan them into this book.... (so we had to be quick before they became rainbow colours!). Both your inputs hastened the process of creating this book considerably!
You are always in our hearts.

THANK YOU!

About the Authors

DR IYA WHITELEY is a training developer for Astronauts with a background in Clinical Psychology and Cognitive Engineering. She designs both equipment and training programmes to improve the performance of highly trained professionals, including military pilots, astronauts, cosmonauts and surgeons. Iya is a Deputy Director of the Centre for Space Medicine at the Mullard Space Science Laboratory, University College London. Iya has worked at the European Astronaut Centre (European Space Agency) in Cologne, Germany and now collaborates with NASA and the Gagarin Cosmonaut Training Centre in Star City, Russia. Since having her own children, Iya now also designs visual books for newborn babies to tap into their developmental potential and give them the best possible start on our unique planet.

DR GRAHAM WHITELEY trained as a Design Engineer. He is a robotics designer and inventor. Graham devises new concepts and realises them using state of the art mechanical and electrical engineering. Graham helped design the world's first five-fingered prosthetic hand which is now worn by thousands of people, making their everyday quality of life that little bit better. The hand won the Da Vinci award and was named one of the top inventions of 2008 by Time Magazine. He has also designed the Schunk SVH, the world's first serially produced anthropomorphic robot hand.

Upcoming titles in the COSMIC BABY BOOKS series
- EARTH DESIGNS: Architecture
- EARTH DESIGNS: The Home Planet and beyond
- EARTH DESIGNS: In The Mouth
- EARTH DESIGNS: Space Exploration

All titles are released to support infants' and children's visual literacy development stages:
Stage 1: From birth - BLACK AND WHITE
Stage 2: From two months old - BLACK AND WHITE AND RED
Stage Infinity: From three years old - COLOURING BOOK

Important to note that all of our titles independent of visual literacy development stages are designed to suit all budding scientists, explorers and artists of all ages.

Authors Support

The authors support La Leche League GB (LLLGB), an affiliate of La Leche League International (LLLI). LLLGB is an nonprofit organisation that provides breastfeeding information and support. As part of LLLI, LLLGB's mission is to help mothers to breastfeed through mother-to-mother support, encouragement, information, and education, and to promote a better understanding of breastfeeding as an important element in the healthy development of the baby and mother.

For each book sold in England and Wales and Northern Ireland Cosmic Baby Books shall donate up to 5% of royalties per book to the La Leche League GB.

For more details see www.laleche.org.uk

Tips for parents on using this book

This book is designed for adults and babies to enjoy together. There are two levels of information- facts for the parent and images for both baby and parent. The book is intended for all ages, presenting interesting images for newborn babies and fascinating facts with accompanying illustrations for primary and secondary school age siblings. Grandparents and great grandparents may equally relish the time spent with their loved ones examining nature's marvels depicted in this book!

The images within this book are inspired by the intricate patterns of some of nature's creatures that live under the sea.

The book and individual images can be used or placed anywhere your baby spends time. Use the book and images, for example:
- In your arms, lying beside you or during tummy time - investigate the book together.
- Next to the cot or nappy-changing mat - place it on the wall or the ceiling once your baby is a bit older.
- In the car – place the book or an image from the book where your baby's gaze will naturally land, such as on or below the headrest, securing it with bulldog clips and string.
- In the kitchen - place an image on the wall opposite your baby's bouncy chair or anywhere the baby is likely to look while being carried over your shoulder.
- In the bath - place an image on the wall to stimulate your baby and keep your baby occupied while dressing them.

A newborn baby can see best at arm's length and as the child develops, they can see further and further away each week. You will need to give your baby about 30 seconds to detect that there is a picture in front of them. So give your baby time to notice the image first. Images can be viewed at any angle, as they are mostly circular and symmetrical in shape. Pick a moment when your baby is calm and receptive, and show a page or two. However, midwives on maternity wards and parents have also reported that black and white images can calm a fidgety newborn baby. Allow an older baby or sibling to flip through the pages themselves. If an older sister or brother is able to read, they may enjoy the images and facts and be encouraged to investigate the topic further or experiment with drawing and colouring their own images. You can read the captions out loud, if you so choose, or describe the picture to your baby in your own words.

If you find other inventive ways of sharing this book with your baby or older sibling, feel free to send us your photo or post it on social media and we will include your ideas in the next edition.

You will notice round dots to the top right of all the images. These dots represent page numbers. The number of dots increases with every page. Your baby will be able to perceive this information better than numbers. It is likely this would be their first introduction to mathematics when images are viewed in order one after another.

We hope you have a wonderful time with your baby studying these intricate, natural patterns.

With love from Cosmic Baby Books, Iya and Graham

The science behind images designed to stimulate a newborn baby

Within their first year, newborns actively rely on their visual perception to learn about the world. A newborn baby is fascinated by patterns and actively seek them out.

When a baby is just born, it has an innate ability to seek out the contrast that faces and eyes provide, which are naturally round in shape and stand out. Your baby learns to recognise you by the oval of your face, as it provides a contrast against your hairline and the background. For example, should you change your hairstyle, let your hair down or tie it back, your baby would need to get used to your new face outline and, in the meantime, recognise you through other senses, such as your smell, touch, taste, or the sound of your voice.

Research has proven that newborns can crawl on their mother's chest to the breast right after birth and successfully feed within an hour of birth. It has been considered that in addition to the odour produced by the breast, the baby seeks out nipples due to their contrast against a mother's skin. The areola and nipple become very dark in pregnant women, which make them stand out like two beacons for the newborn to home in on.

We know from laboratory tests of newborns' gaze that young babies prefer highly contrasting images. At first black and white images attract the most attention. From two months babies begin to see their first colour - red. We also know a newborn baby prefers rounded shapes and find it easier to trace them, as their eye muscles have not had much practice at making sharp movements.

Newborns' attention when stimulated first via black and white images can increase from a few seconds to one and half minutes in just one week. A longer attention span allows for greater learning. From two months a red colour can be introduced. With practice, your baby will study the environment and information for longer and more thoroughly, creating new neural pathways and reinforcing established ones.

Studies show that very young babies can differentiate more than a dozen stripes in one square inch of an image. They need time (about half a minute) to actually choose to look at the object. As a rule, early in their development babies can only see as far as their hands can reach and subsequently see further and further away every week. By the time babies become toddlers and are able to walk, their vision is well developed to support them in exploring the world at large.

Our black and white books for newborns and babies are based on current scientific findings on newborns' and babies' visual perception and brain development. The images within our books help:
- improve concentration through stimulating and captivating images.
- stimulate further learning and discovery.
- create new pathways in the brain through learning to trace visual patterns.
- acquire early life skills required for successful learning and interaction.

ASTEROBLASTUS STELLATUS
facts by cosmic baby books

Asteroblastus stellatus is an ancestor of the Sea Lily; the animal that looks like a starfish on a stalk. They were around over 450 million years ago when fish with jaws were about to appear. With this new threat *Blastoid* creatures evolved the ability to regenerate. Surviving Sea Lilies possess ancestoral skeletal five-sector symmetry and similarly attach themselves to the rocky bottom by a stalk.

The Sea Lily mostly eats suspended particles in the water that float by, such as plankton. It uses grooves within its five radiating petals to capture food. These work like tiny conveyors delivering food into its mouth in the centre.

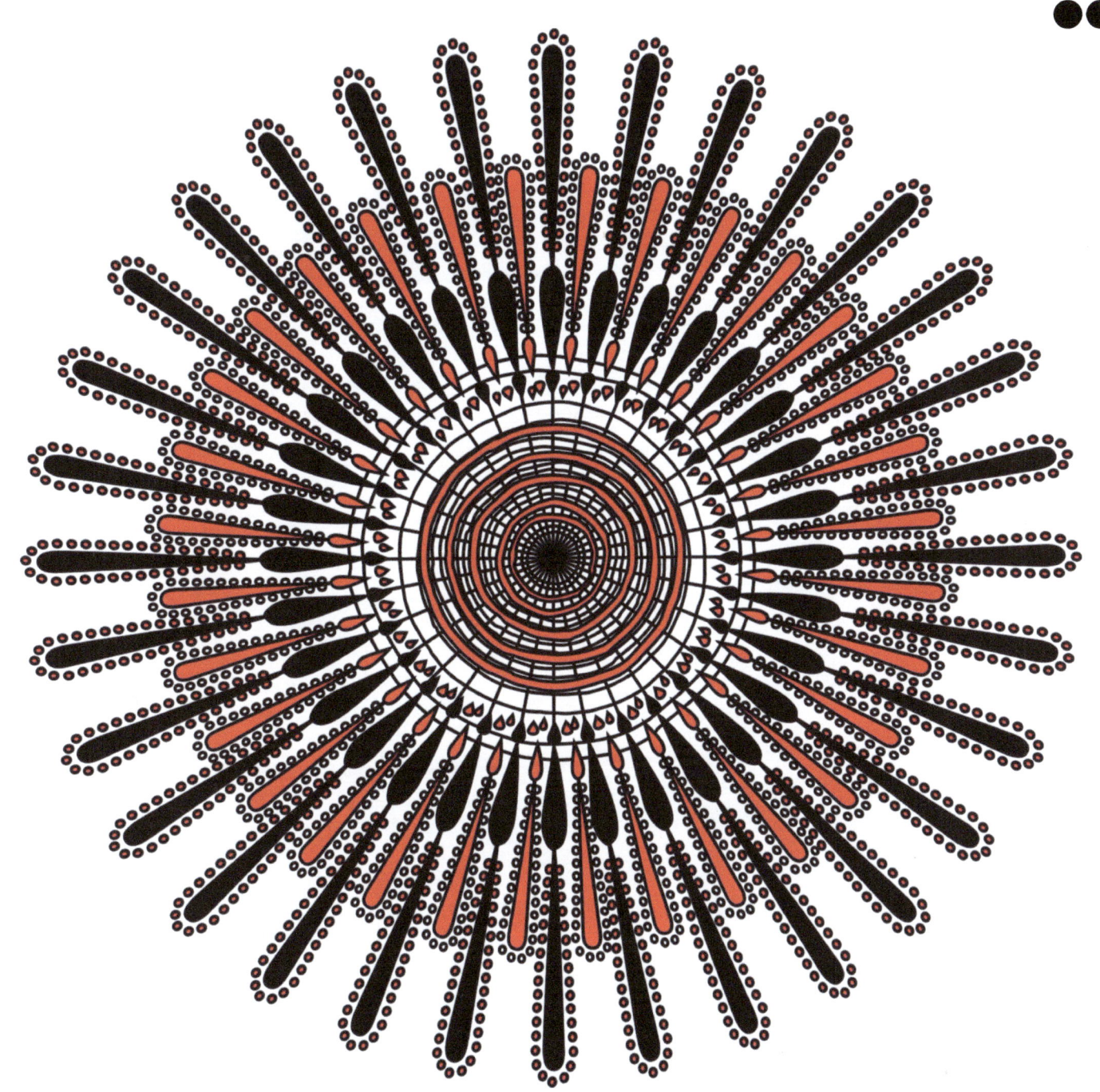

PORPITA PRUNELLA
facts by cosmic baby books

Commonly known as the blue button jellyfish, but it is not really a jellyfish. Actually, it is a colony of carnivores! These are called hydroids, a relative of the jellyfish. Surrounded by other small animals called zooids that form tentacles with stinging knobs at their ends called nematocysts.

These tiny individual animals live together harmoniously by performing specific roles. One variety has radiating tentacles to catch prey, reproduce and digest. Other clusters of individuals keep the colony afloat by creating a gas-filled disc in the middle which is hardened by chitinous material.

Chitin is so strong and flexible that it is used as surgical thread. Due to its natural biodegradable properties it dissolves, and has even been found to accelerate the healing of wounds.

POLIOPOGON AMADOU

facts by cosmic baby books

This animal is composed of thousands of silica needles, called spicule. Consequently, its common name is Glass Sponge. It grows into a tall vase form becoming home to a monogamous shrimp couple that enters this Glass 'house' to remain there for the rest of their lives. Only their tiny offspring can eventually leave this home, through small windows of this Glass house.

In Japan, this vase-like animal symbolises eternal love and are given as wedding gifts.

The extraordinary structures of the Glass house are studied by architects to improve structural performance and flexibility of buildings.

BOTRYLLUS
facts by cosmic baby books

Botryllus schlosseri is between 2-4mm in diameter and squirts water if disturbed, hence the name, the sea-squirt! The star-like pattern of the colony, called the 'test', inspired its common name the Golden Star Tunicate. A colony of sea-squirts is covered in a jelly and would fit in your palm.

Each zooid generates a current of water through pulsating cilia, the tiny hairs inside their bodies. As a result, water saturated with plankton is attracted to the mouth opening where food is trapped in mucus which then passes to the stomach. Once digested the remains are passed into a common chamber shared by the whole colony.

Botryllus loves sheltered areas like ship docks, and are very common around the coasts of Britain

CASSIOPEA ANDROMEDA

facts by cosmic baby books

In Turkey this is called the alien jellyfish. It often invades tourist lagoons, lying at the bottom of muddy, marshy shallow water. Lying upside down with its mouth upwards, it vibrates its arms to bring food to its mouth. Whilst its appearance pretends to be a benign sea anemone, it is in fact a poisonous jellyfish.

Its scientific name references the Greek myth of Queen Cassiopeia and her daughter Andromeda. In the story, Andromeda is chained to the rocks and destined to be eaten by the sea monster until rescued by the greatest Greek hero, Perseus. After an adventure beheading the Gorgon Medusa, he saves Andromeda on the winged horse Pegasus. All ends well; they marry, have beautiful children, and live happily ever after.

HEMIPHOLIS CORDIFERA
facts by cosmic baby books

This is a picture of a mouth on the central disc portion of a starfish skeleton, commonly known as a Brittle Starfish. In the living creature 5 long arms sprawl outward from this disc. The Brittle Star possesses the ability to regenerate its lost arms and even part of the damaged disc, hence its name!

Its mouth, with 5 jaws, is on the underside of the disc, which is also their bottom! They can capture food by raising their body onto their arms and trapping food in a mucus net spread between the spines of their arms.

Some species of brittle stars are bioluminescent and emit light

CENTROSTEPHANUS LONGISPINUS
facts by cosmic baby books

Centrostephanus longispinus literally means long-spine sea-urchin. In fact, the spines are around three times longer than their body. These long needle-like spines have a cell structure that can change conformation, enabling it to change to a different hue in response to a change in its surroundings - camouflage. When in shallow water in a hot country, these urchins manage to hold up seaweed or even shells on long finger-like spines to make an umbrella to hide from the hot sun!

As they are rather prickly, procreation happens outside their bodies; entailing the simultaneous release of eggs and sperm into the water. This is coordinated by the urchins releasing a chemical pheromone, so that the neighbouring urchin can sense that it is baby making season

NAUTILUS POMPILIUS
facts by cosmic baby books

Nautili have inhabited the Earth since about 500 million years ago, even before dinosaurs. They are considered to be 'living fossils' as they look the same as they did these millions of years ago.

A nautilus dives just like a submarine. It uses an argon - nitrogen gas filled shell chamber to regulate its buoyancy and empties its 'dive-tanks' to descend. It travels up to the surface from a depth of 2000 feet at sunset to feed and then goes back down again at sunrise.

The nautilus incubation period is as long as a human baby's! It ranges from nine months to over a year.

HAECKELIANA PORCELLANA
facts by cosmic baby books

Haeckeliana porcellana is a zooplankton floating in abundance across our seas and oceans. Being so small, at less than half a millimetre in diameter (about as thick as a baby's thumb nail), it is classed as a nanoplankton.

It is named 'Porcellana', due to its exquisite silica-built exoskeleton, the same material used to create very fine translucent china.

Silica is vital to our healthy teeth, bones, nails, blood vessels and more. The best source for it is oats, but we can also obtain it from water and bread, mangos and bananas, spinach and even beer!

CANNORRHIZA CONNEXA
facts by cosmic baby books

This jellyfish has eight frilly oral arms instead of a mouth and lacks tentacles on the bell's rim. It belongs to the order of jellyfish called Rhizostomae, which translated from the Greek means 'roots from the mouth'. Their mouth is fused. They eat like a sponge via suctorial minimouths, located all along these oral arms. As Rhizostomae do not have tentacles, that other jellyfish use to capture prey, they use tiny arrow cells to immobilise their prey or eat whatever just happened to pass through their oral arms.

This variety of jellyfish is edible and very popular in Japan and China. It is also fished for its medicinal properties.

NAUSITHOE CHALLENGERI

facts by cosmic baby books

This tiny jellyfish, just over 10 mm wide, belongs to a class of immortal beings! This animal can regress to its younger form and regenerate again and again. It is an evolved form of survival.

In their mature form they can reproduce through sharing eggs and sperm. However; if life becomes tough and the environment is threatening their survival, they can drop to the floor of the ocean, become younger selves, and grow as a polyp in a colony that looks like long stalks. When the time is right, they just slice or bud themselves off the stalk and swim away to enjoy single life again.

The later process is called a reverse ontogeny

SOLMARIS
facts by cosmic baby books

This miniature jellyfish is a width of your thumb nail and possesses a truly invisible cloak that is transparent like the water it inhabits. *Solmaris* wears its stomach like a hula-hoop; as tube that runs around the entire edge of the jellyfish umbrella. The outermost 'skin' of the jellyfish umbrella is named the exumbrella. Solmaris sense organs and exumbrellar are fluorescent. They light up under the blue to ultraviolet light range.

The green fluorescent protein gene was first isolated in a jellyfish and since has been introduced into many organisms; from bacteria to fungi, plants, flies and even mammalian and human cells. This gene can also be passed on to the next generation.

All images are hand drawn with our wonderful newborn baby boy sleeping or feeding in our arms and then edited using a software for crispiness required for a newborn baby. All images are inspired by:

ASTEROBLASTUS STELLATUS: Haeckel, Ernst (1904). Kunstformen der Natur. Plate 80, page 325, figure 11a.

PORPITA PRUNELLA: Haeckel, Ernst (1904). Kunstformen der Natur. Plate 17, page 115, figure 5.

POLIOPOGON AMADOU: Haeckel, Ernst (1904). Kunstformen der Natur. Plate 35, page 172, figure 8.

BOTRYLLUS: Haeckel, Ernst (1904). Kunstformen der Natur. Plate 85, page 344, figure 9.

CASSIOPEA ANDROMEDA (*Cassiopeja cyclobalia*): Haeckel, Ernst (1904). Kunstformen der Natur. Plate 28, page 147, figure 6. Previously it was known as *Cassiopeja cyclobalia*, now known as Cassiopea andromeda. https://www.mba.ac.uk/nmbl/publications/jmba_40/Rhizostomeae.pdf

HEMIPHOLIS CORDIFERA: Haeckel, Ernst (1904). Kunstformen der Natur. Plate 70, page 291, figure 7.

CENTROSTEPHANUS LONGISPINUS: Haeckel, Ernst (1904). Kunstformen der Natur. Plate 60, page 258, figure 9.

NAUTILUS POMPILIUS: Nautilus pompilius by Joop Trausel and Frans Slieker, Natural History Museum Rotterdam. Creative Commons Attribution-Share Alike 4.0 International license. Accessed through: World Register of Marine Species (WoRMS) at http://www.marinespecies.org/photogallery.php?album=701&pic=75788

HAECKELIANA PORCELLANA: Haeckel, Ernst (1904). Kunstformen der Natur. Plate 1, page 65, figure 3a.

CANNORRHIZA CONNEXA: Haeckel, Ernst (1904). Kunstformen der Natur. Plate 88, page 355, figure 7.

NAUSITHOE CHALLENGERI: Haeckel, Ernst (1904). Kunstformen dr Natur. Plate 18, page 118, figure 8.

SOLMARIS: Haeckel, Ernst (1904). Kunstformen der Natur. Plate 16, page 112, figure 4.

Wonderful Activities for you and your baby to enjoy

Try dancing with your baby to your favourite music. Go on! Show your best moves and see how your baby responds. Baby will feel you enjoying the music and movement. It is likely to relax you and the baby and may make a connection between you in yet another unique way. Try holding your baby in different holds, your baby might prefer some holds more than others. You are the best and the most favourite person in your baby's life. Most importantly, HAVE FUN!

These are your baby's first social experiences of connecting with you and their surrounding environment. It is a wonderful encouragement for your baby to learn and to experiment with you.

On the following two pages all twelve images are presented in a smaller size. You are welcome to laminate them and cut them out. You can carry them in your bag and enjoy playing with your baby when you are out and about.

***

Have you had fun with your baby looking through this book in the Earth Design series?

If you did, we would love to read your review. This will encourage and inspire us to draw more, to discover more facts and to design more books. Also, every positive review encourages other families to experience these books!

If you would like to discover more themes in the Earth Design series with your baby, sign up to our newsletter via our website, connect with us on Facebook @cosmicbabybooks and Instagram #cosmicbabybooks.

Tag and share your baby photos reading our books with #cosmicbabybooks to win books and special gifts in our monthly competitions.

cosmicbabybooks.com

We value your feedback and much appreciate your support!

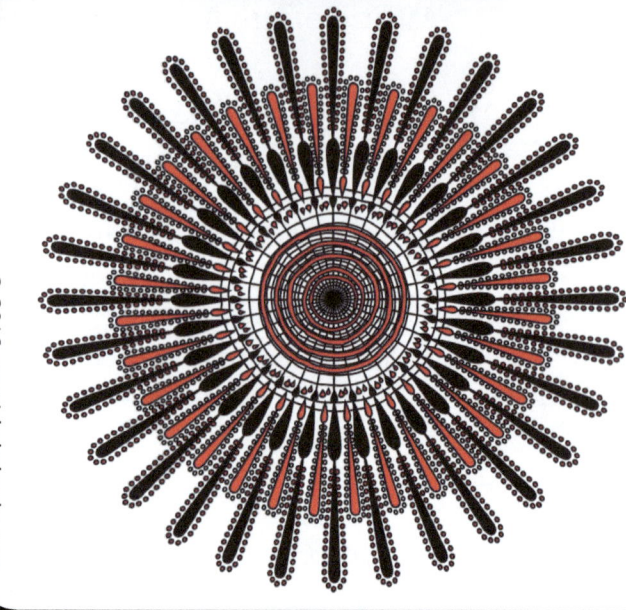

www.ingramcontent.com/pod-product-compliance
Lightning Source LLC
Chambersburg PA
CBHW042254100526
44587CB00003B/131